T0344044

Welcome 2

1 My birthday 4

2 At school 11

3 My family 18

4 My body 25

5 Pets 32

6 My house 39

7 Food 46

8 I'm happy! 53

Picture dictionary 60

Festivals 62

1 Match and trace.

Beth   Cody   Waldo   Harry

2 Trace. Then colour.

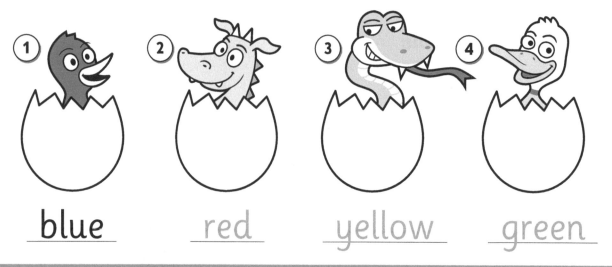

blue   red   yellow   green

 **3** Trace. Then count and match.

1   2   3   4   5

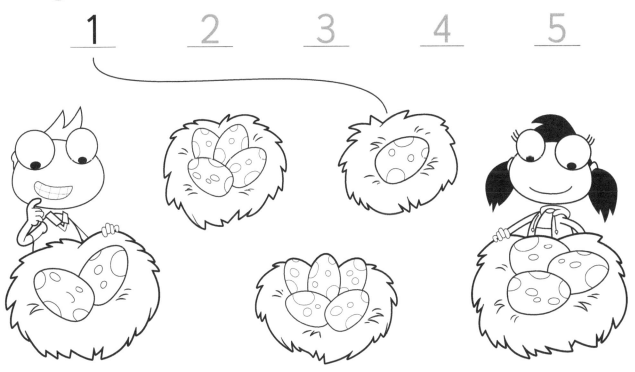

 **4** Colour and say. Then trace and match.

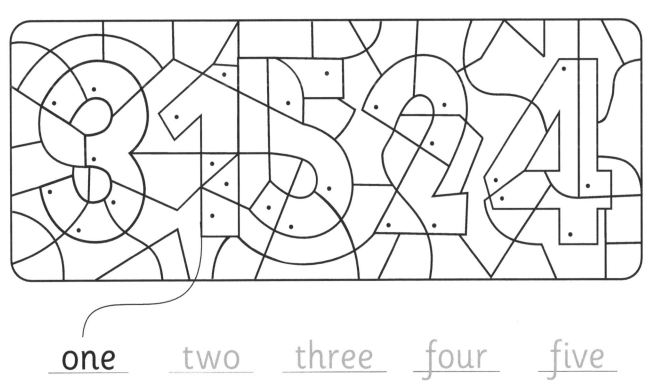

one   two   three   four   five

1 My birthday

Trace and colour.

1 pink

2 orange

3 black

4 brown

5 purple

6 white

7 grey

2 Trace. Then count, write and match.

six   seven   eight   nine   ten

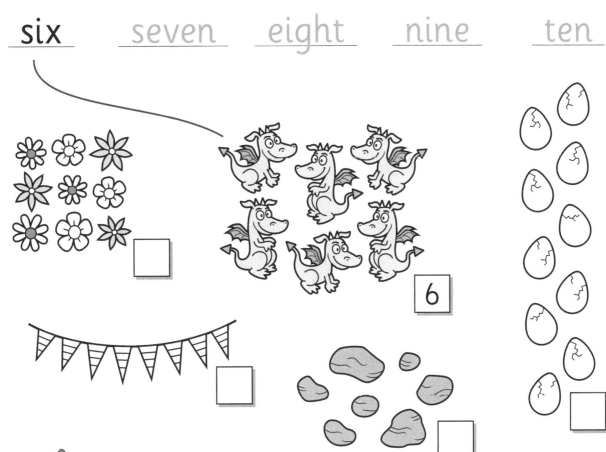

3 Join the dots.

I'm a dragon.

5  **Trace and say.**

I'm nine.

6   **Trace. Then listen and colour.**

b

p

7   **Trace and colour. Then write and colour.**

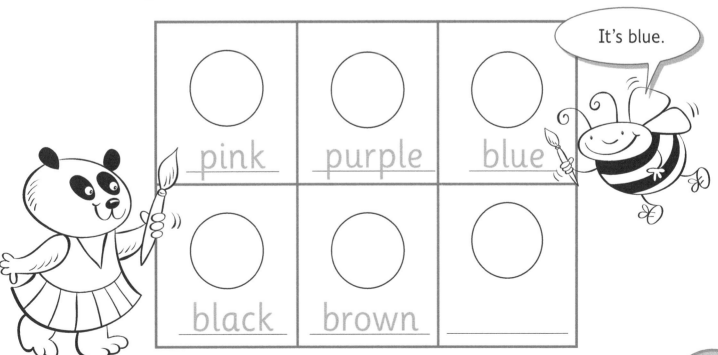

It's blue.

pink   purple   blue

black   brown

Listen and circle. Then colour.

1
a    b    **2** a    b

3
a    b

   Count and write. Then say.

a  8

b

c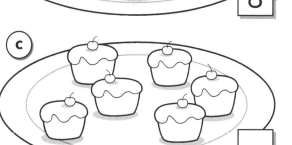

d

10 Match. Then trace.

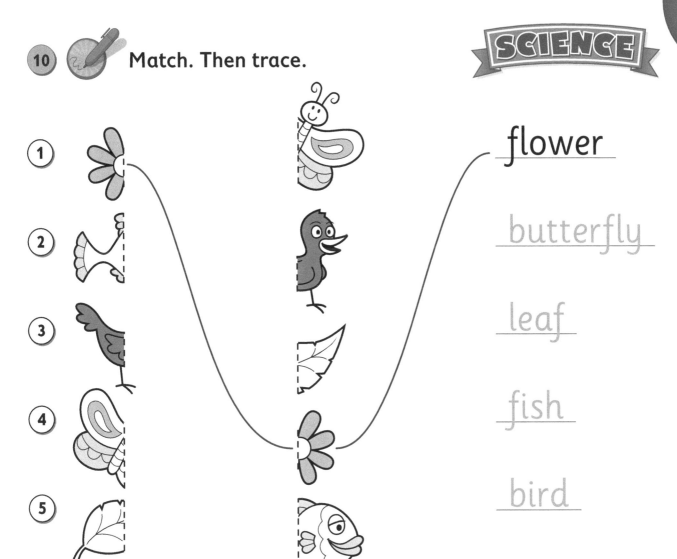

flower

butterfly

leaf

fish

bird

11 Colour. Then circle.

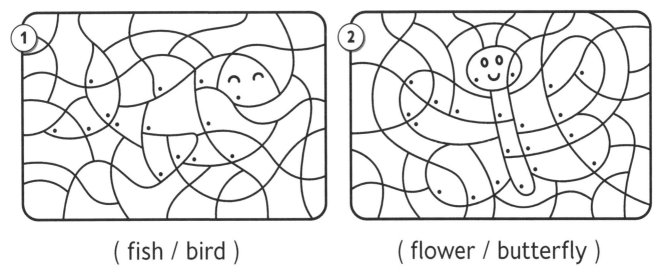

(fish / bird)   (flower / butterfly)

Read and colour.

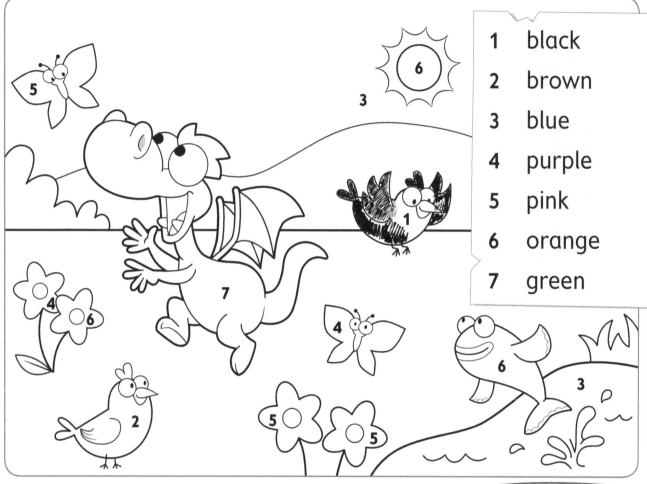

1 black
2 brown
3 blue
4 purple
5 pink
6 orange
7 green

13 **Draw and write. Then say.**

2 At school

1 Draw. Then trace.

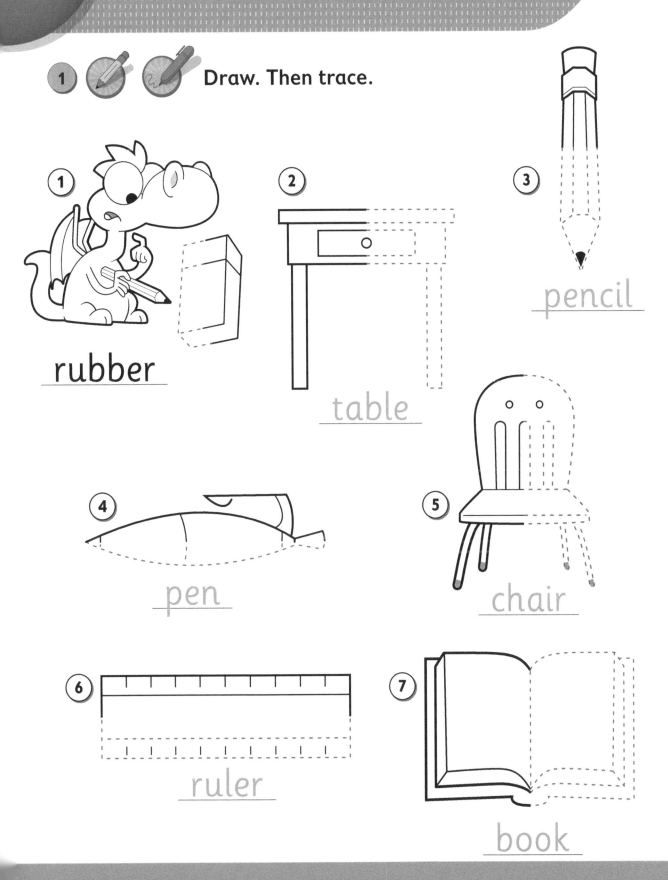

1 rubber

2 table

3 pencil

4 pen

5 chair

6 ruler

7 book

 **2** Find and circle. Then say.

1

2

3 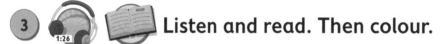 Listen and read. Then colour.

a yellow rubber

a green book

a red ruler

a black chair

a pink pencil

a brown table

a purple pen

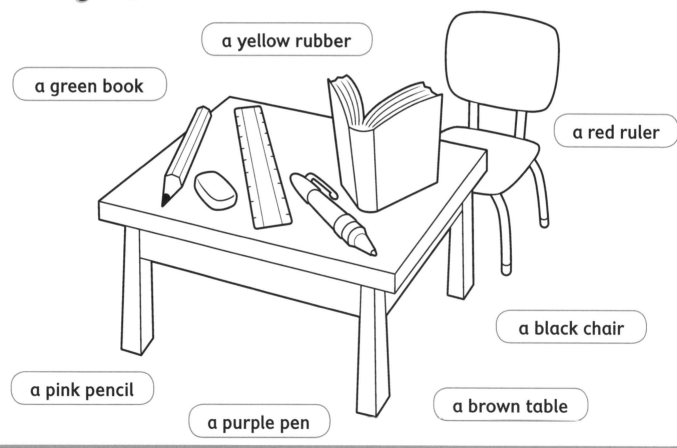

4  **Listen and draw.**

1
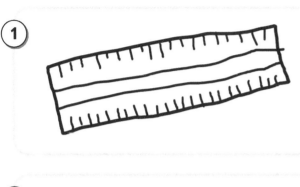

2

3

4

5  **Find and count. Then write and trace.**

4	rubbers

☐ pencils

☐ rulers

☐ books

Trace. Then listen, match and colour.

l = yellow   r = red

   Join the dots. Then trace and say.

•4   6•

3•   •7

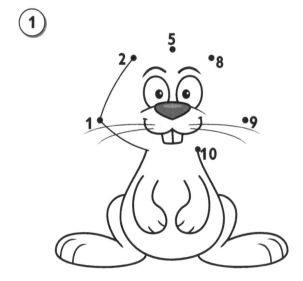

① 5 2• •8 1• •9 •10

rabbit

② 1 2 •3 •4 •5 6• 10• 9• 8• 7•

lamb

8  Listen and number.

 STORY

a

b

1

c

d

9   Draw. Then trace and colour.

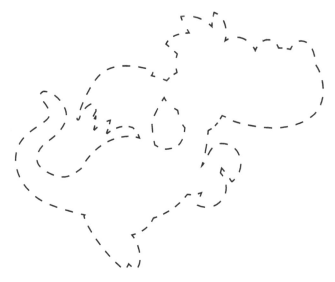

A _green_ dragon.

10   **Match and trace. Then say.**

1  2  3  4

piano   **guitar**   drum   violin

11   **Read and circle.**

1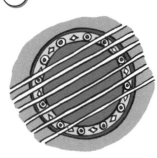

2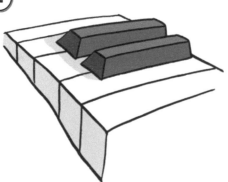

3

(guitar / drum)   (piano / violin)   (piano / drum)

 **Read and match.**

pencils

pens

book

rubber

rulers

table

chair

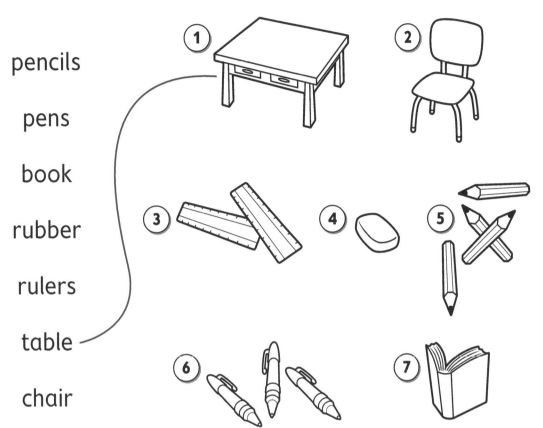

13 **Read and colour.**

a red pencil

a blue book

1 Trace. Then match and say.

1 mum

2 dad

3 granny

4 grandad

5 brother

6 sister

This is my family .

2 Find and colour. Then circle.

(nine / ten)

(seven / eight)

   3 Look and match. Then say.

 **4** Listen and ✔ or ✘.

1 ✔

2 ☐

3 ☐

4 ☐

5  Trace. Then match and say.

happy   sad

6  Trace. Then listen and match.

7 Count. Then write and trace.

① seals

② zebras

 **8** Read. Then circle.

1 my mum
   a   b

2 my dad
   a   b

3 my aunt
   a   b

9  Trace and colour.

This is my ___sister___ .
She's ___six___ .

10  Listen and number.
Then trace.

a   b   c   d

1

doctor   teacher   vet   pilot

11 Read and match.

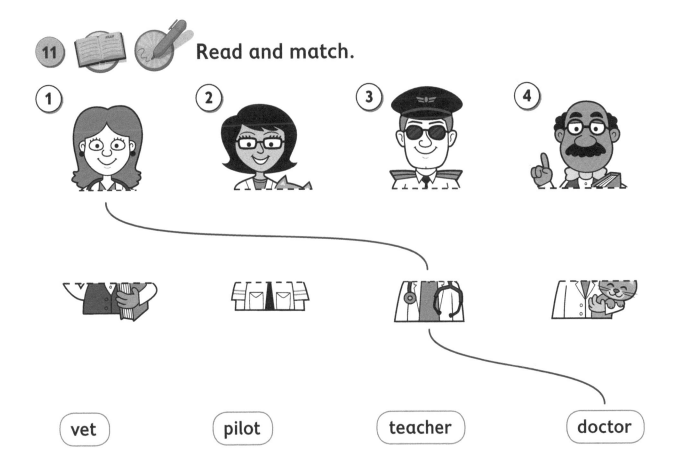

1   2   3   4

vet   pilot   teacher   doctor

12   **Read and number.**

1. dad   2. mum   3. granny

My family.

4. grandad   5. sister   6. brother

13  **Trace and circle.**

LOOK!

my granny
my sister

4 My body

1 Trace. Then number.

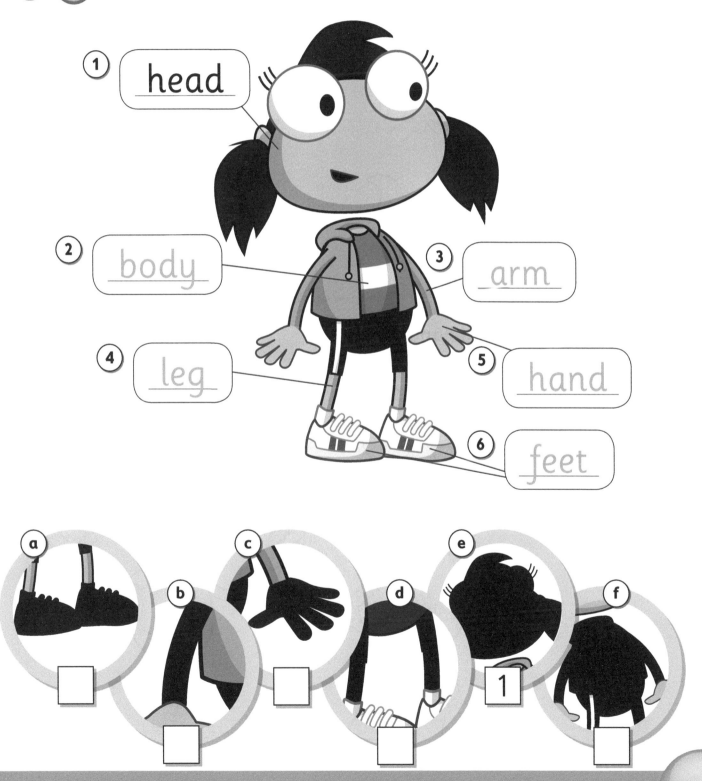

1 head

2 body

3 arm

4 leg

5 hand

6 feet

a

b

c

d

e 1

f

2 Trace. Then find and circle.

1 _feet_

2 _wings_

3 _tail_

3   **Read and colour.**

I've got a purple body.

I've got orange hands.

4  Count and trace. Then write and say.

I've got three legs.

☐ fingers

☐ arms

3 legs

☐ toes

☐ feet

5   2:08 Listen and say *Yes* or *No*.

Trace. Then listen and circle.

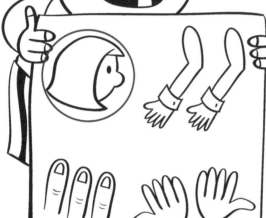

7   **Draw. Then trace and say.**

1

I've got a ___guitar___.

2

I've got two ___hands___.

Draw and ✔ or ✗.

1 I've got 2 heads. ☐

2 I've got 3 legs. ☐

3 I've got 4 arms. ☐

   Listen and draw. Then say.

 **Read and match.**

a I've got dirty feet.

b I've got clean hands.

c Wash your hands.

d I've got dirty hands.

1 d

2

3

4

11  **Draw. Then read and circle.**

I've got (1 / ②) heads.

(4 / 5) arms
(6 / 8) fingers
(2 / 3) legs
(5 / 6) toes

LOOK!

12   **Read and colour.**

I've got blue legs.

I've got a yellow body.

Lesson 7

31

5 Pets

1 **Find. Then trace.**

1

parrot

2

cat

3

dog

4

frog

5

rabbit

6

mouse

7

tortoise

 **2** Read and match. Then say.

It's big.

It's small.

 3 Find and circle the odd one out.

①

②

③

Listen and circle.

1

2

  Read and write.

1 He's got a rabbit.   **2** She's got a frog.

3 He's got a dog.   **4** She's got a cat.

a

b

c

d

1

Sing. (See Pupil's Book page 38.)

 **6** Trace. Then listen and ✔.

SOUNDS FUN!

d

✔

t

7 Trace. Then circle and say.

dog   dad   drum

d = green   t = blue

two   ten   tortoise

8   **Listen and number.**

a

b

c

1

d

9  **Draw and ✔.**

He's got a...   dog [ ]   cat [ ]   rabbit [ ]

10 **Trace. Then match.**

 SCIENCE

puppy

kitten

chick

 11   **Join the dots. Then circle and say.**

1 It's a chick. (Yes / No)

2 It's a kitten. (Yes / No)

12 **Read and write.**

cat frog mouse parrot rabbit tortoise

He's got a...

<u>dog</u> _____

_____ _____

She's got a...

<u>cat</u> _____

_____ _____

LOOK!

13 **Read and circle.**

He's got a (frog / mouse / rabbit).

1 Draw. Then trace.

2 door

3 window

1 bedroom

4 bathroom

5 kitchen

6 dining room

7 living room

 **Read and match.**

1

2

She's in the bathroom.

He's in the dining room.

He's in the kitchen.

She's in the living room.

3

4

 **Join the dots. Then circle and say.**

He's in the (bedroom / living room).

4 Find and count.

in the garden	☐
in the bedroom	☐
in the bathroom	☐

5  Trace. Then read and draw.

It's in the ___garden___ .   It's in the ___bed___ .   It's in the ___bath___ .

6 **Trace. Then listen and circle.**

SOUNDS FUN!

1 V

 drum

 garden

 violin

2 W

 guitar

 window

 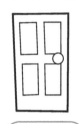 door

7 **Find and colour in green or blue.**

v = green

w = blue

8   **Listen and number. Then match.**

a

b

c 1

d

9   **Read and ✓ or ✗.**

1

2

3

He's in the
kitchen.

He's in the
living room.

He's in the
bathroom.

Lesson 5

10 📖 🎧 2:48 **Read. Then listen and draw.**

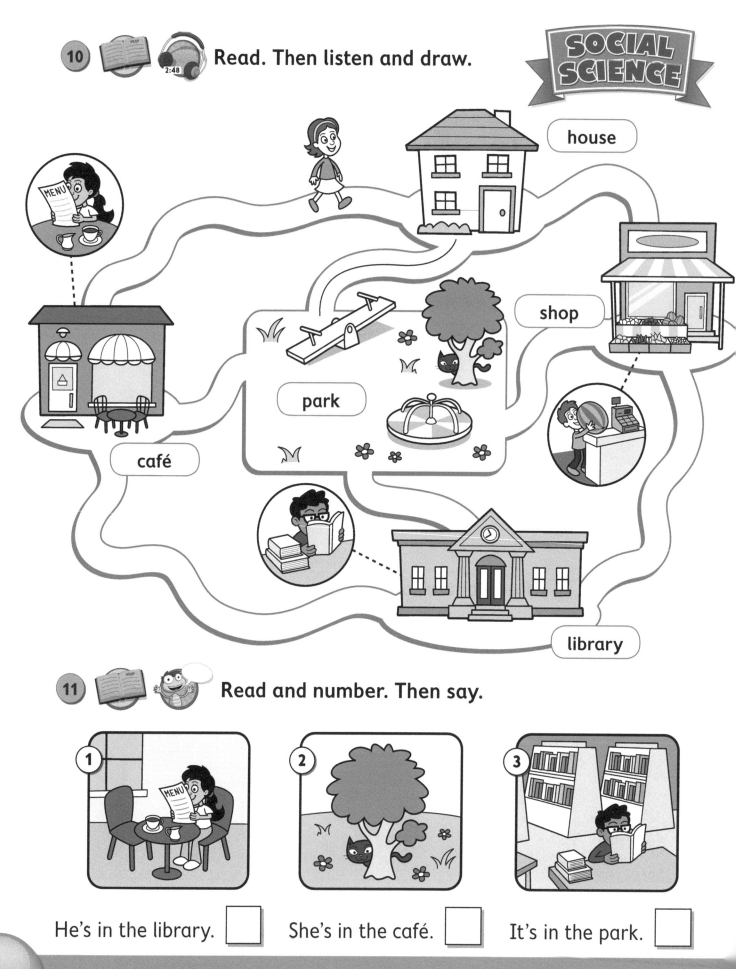

house

shop

park

café

library

11 📖 😃 **Read and number. Then say.**

1

2

3

He's in the library. ☐   She's in the café. ☐   It's in the park. ☐

12  **Read and write.**

| bathroom | bedroom | ~~kitchen~~ | living room |

1

She's in the _____**kitchen**_____.

2

He's in the _____.

3

He's in the _____.

4

She's in the _____.

13  **Read and circle.**

LOOK!

She's in the (bedroom / garden / dining room).

7 Food

1  Draw. Then trace.

1
bread

2
yoghurt

3
milk

4
cheese

5
fruit

6
fish

7
salad

8
cake

2 **Find and colour. Then read and ✔.**

salad ☐

fish ☐

yoghurt ☐

fruit ☐

bread ☐

milk ☐

cheese ☐

cake ☐

I like...

3   **Read and draw.**

I like yoghurt, bread and cheese.

 **Circle the odd one out.**
Then listen and check.

 ①

②

  Read and number.

1 I like honey.   **2** I like bread.

3 I don't like jelly.   **4** I don't like cheese.

6   **Trace. Then listen and play bingo.**

I like _jelly_ .

I like _yoghurt_ .

  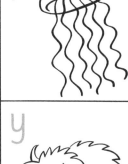

7   **Trace and colour.**

① juice

② yoghurt

③ jelly

④ yellow

8 **Read and match.**

1 I like apples.
2 I like ice cream.

a

b

c HONEY

d

9 **Read and draw. Then say.**

I like...
milk   fish
fruit   bread

I don't like...
cheese

10  **Find and trace.**

1

2

3

chocolate

cake

salad

11 **Read and ✔. Then draw.**

It's good for me!

fruit ☐

salad ☐

cake ☐

bread ☐

yoghurt ☐

fish ☐

chocolate ☐

 **Find. Then read and write.**

| bread | cake | honey |
| jelly | milk | yoghurt |

(1) (2) (3)

MILK

I like...

bread

(4) (5) (6)

I don't like...

LOOK!

13  **Read and ✔.**

I like cheese. ☐

I like fish. ☐

MILK

Yoghurt

8 I'm happy!

  Look and trace.

I'm __scared__ .

I'm __tired__ .

I'm __happy__ .

I'm __hungry__ .

I'm __thirsty__ .

2 Listen and ✔ or ✗.

1 ✔ 2 ☐ 3 ☐ 4 ☐

3 Find. Then read and circle.

1 She's (happy / (tired)).

2 He's (thirsty / tired).

3 He's (happy / thirsty).

4 She's (scared / hungry).

5 He's (happy / hungry).

Chant. (See Pupil's Book page 61.)

 **SONG**

4  Match.

① ② ③ ④

stamp   jump   clap   turn around

5 Read. Then circle in green or blue.

drink = green

eat = blue

HONEY

6 Trace and colour.

sh = blue

ch = green

7 Circle the odd one out. Then listen and check.

1

chocolate

shadow

chair

2

cheese

shell

shark

Listen and number.

 **Draw and write.** (hungry thirsty tired)

I'm _____.

I'm _____.

1 It's a big shadow. ☐

2 It's a small shadow. ☐

3 It's a big shadow. ☐

11 Read and circle.

① It's a (table / (chair)).

② It's a (hand / head).

③ It's a (frog / butterfly).

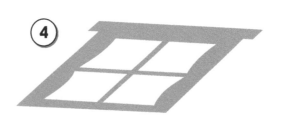

④ It's a (window / door).

Find. Then read and write.

| happy | hungry | scared | thirsty | ~~tired~~ |

1 He's ___tired___ .

2 He's _____ .

3 She's _____ .

4 She's _____ .

5 He's _____ .

LOOK!

13 **Read and ✔.**

I'm sad. ☐

I'm tired. ☐

I'm hungry. ☐

Picture dictionary

Colours

red yellow green blue pink purple orange brown black white grey

Numbers

one two three four five six seven eight nine ten

Classroom objects

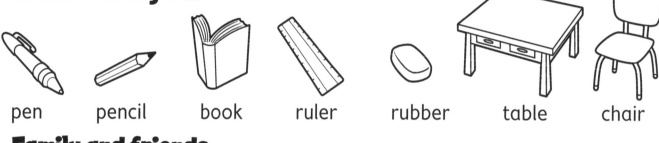

pen pencil book ruler rubber table chair

Family and friends

mum dad brother sister friend granny grandad aunt

My body

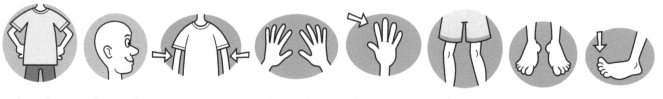

body head arms hands fingers legs feet toes

Animals

dog   cat   rabbit   parrot   mouse   tortoise   frog

In the house

house   dining room   kitchen   living room

bedroom   bathroom   door   window

Food and drink

salad   fruit   bread   cheese   yoghurt   milk   fish   cake

Feelings

happy   sad   scared   tired   hungry   thirsty

1 Match. Then trace.

witch   pumpkin   cat   **monster**   bat

2 Join the dots. Then circle.

(monster / pumpkin / witch)

Christmas

1  Trace and match. Then listen and colour.

sleigh present reindeer Santa

2 Draw. Then write and trace.

To _____
Happy
Christmas!
From Santa.

1 Trace. Then colour and write.

 bunny   chick   egg

It's an _____.

2 Look and draw.